3/10

D0712877

Poltergeists

HAL MARCOVITZ

THE LIBRARY OF
Ghosts & Hauntings

ReferencePoint
Press®

San Diego, CA

ABOUT THE AUTHOR
Hal Marcovitz is a former newspaper reporter who once participated in a séance and helped the Philadelphia Ghost Hunters Alliance search for a poltergeist at the Bucksville Inn. He has written more than 120 books for young readers. He makes his home in Chalfont, Pennsylvania, with his wife, Gail, and daughter Ashley.

Picture credits:
Cover: iStockphoto.com
AP Images: 33, 35, 67
iStockphoto.com: 7, 53, 63
Landov: 59
North Wind: 39
Photoshot: 11, 15, 19, 27, 48, 55, 71
Science Photo Library: 50, 69

Series design and book layout:
Amy Stirnkorb

LIBRARY OF CONGRESS CATALOGING-IN-PUBLICATION DATA

Marcovitz, Hal.
 Poltergeists / by Hal Marcovitz.
  p. cm. -- (The library of ghosts and hauntings)
 Includes bibliographical references and index.
 ISBN-13: 978-1-60152-093-7 (hardback)
 ISBN-10: 1-60152-093-X (hardback)
 1. Poltergeists--Juvenile literature. I. Title.
 BF1483.M37 2009
 133.1'42--dc22
                                                    2009010036

Contents

Introduction

What Is a Poltergeist?

Soon after graduating from high school, Carole Compton left her home in Scotland to work as a nanny for a wealthy Italian family in Rome. After Compton moved in to the family's home, though, a strange thing happened. As the young nanny walked past a framed picture on the wall, it fell to the floor, the glass smashing at her feet. A few days later, as Compton accompanied the family on a holiday in the Italian Alps, a fire broke out in the home. A fire company quickly responded and doused the flames, but as the firefighters searched through the home, they could find no explanation for what caused the blaze. During the next few days, additional fires broke out in the house—including one in the bedroom of the family's baby. Suspicious that Compton might be an arsonist, the family dismissed her.

Compton found another job as a nanny, and soon a fire broke out in that family's home as well. Within a few days, the family was forced to endure other strange occurrences—a statue on the property was found toppled over and smashed; loud, unexplainable noises often erupted in the home; an expensive vase suddenly

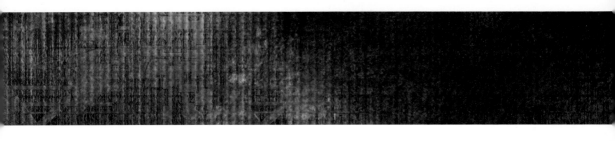

and without apparent reason toppled over and fell to the floor, smashing into dozens of pieces. When a second fire erupted in the house, family members called police. It did not take long for the Italian police to investigate and learn that suspicious fires seemed to follow Compton from job to job. She was arrested and charged with attempted murder and arson. The Italian press learned of the other strange events that occurred around Compton and labeled her a *strega*—Italian for "witch."

News stories about Compton soon came to the attention of paranormal investigators, who examined the evidence and concluded that Compton was not an arsonist; nor did they believe she was a witch. Rather, the paranormal experts suspected very strongly that the young Scottish woman was the victim of a poltergeist.

Noisy Ghost

The term *poltergeist* comes from the combination of two German words—*polter,* which means to knock or make loud noises, and *geist,* which means "ghost." Therefore, a poltergeist is a noisy ghost. But a poltergeist is much more than a noisy nuisance. As the Carole Compton case would indicate, a poltergeist is a ghost that causes mischief—and sometimes the mischief of a poltergeist can be potentially deadly. "The poltergeist is a noisy, mischievous, destructive entity prone to acts of mindless violence,"[1] says author and paranormal investigator Brian Righi.

Typically, the poltergeist's pranks manifest themselves

in unexplainable noises or objects that fly through the air, seemingly under their own power, or other weird happenings—such as fires breaking out without cause. In most cases a poltergeist does not reveal itself as an apparition would, but occasionally people who claim to have undergone experiences with poltergeists say they saw physical manifestations of the spirits as well as other unworldly images.

As the Compton case also shows, poltergeists often attach themselves to people and follow them from place to place. Unlike other ghosts, which may move in to a house and stay there for hundreds of years, haunting whoever lives there, the poltergeist seems to be drawn to the energy of a specific person. This person is regarded as the poltergeist's human agent. Moreover, victims of poltergeist possession are often young women or girls. (Compton was just out of high school when she started attracting the poltergeist's attention.) Paranormal investigators suspect that young women and girls give off an energy as they approach maturity that spirits find irresistible. Others argue that there is a scientific explanation for the "pranks" of the poltergeist—that the human agents, particularly young women and girls, harbor an otherwise deeply hidden power known as recurrent spontaneous psychokinesis, or RSPK, which gives them the ability to levitate objects.

Meanwhile, there are also cases on record of poltergeists attaching themselves to men and boys as well as instances in which poltergeists move in to a house and stay there, delightfully haunting whoever happens to stop by. Many houses and other places haunted by poltergeists have been the scenes of grisly murders or other tragic events, but in many cases paranormal investigators have been stumped as to why the poltergeist picked

a particular place to stir up mischief. By their nature poltergeists revel in their unpredictability.

Contradictory Evidence

As for Carole Compton, paranormal investigators offered to testify on her behalf, but Compton's attorneys decided to keep their testimony out of the case, believing that a defense based on the existence of a poltergeist would not help matters. Besides, the prosecutor's case featured an abundance of contradictory evidence. Arson investigators testified that a mattress she was alleged to have set on fire somehow ignited from a heat source *inside* the mattress, rather than from someone taking a match to it. In another case the flames seemed to burn *down* toward the floor rather than up toward the ceiling—an impossible circumstance fire investigators found themselves unable to explain. Still the Italian court found her guilty of arson, although the court acquitted her on the charge of attempted murder. She was then freed. Compton had spent 16 months in jail prior to the trial; the court gave her credit for time served and let her go.

Following the trial, Compton moved to England, married, and started raising her own family. She has never been bothered by a poltergeist again, but retains vivid memories of her harrowing experiences in Italy. "What happened to me is something that never goes away," she said. "It was a dreadful ordeal."[2]

Did You Know?
People who die in fires often reappear as poltergeists. Clues to their identities can often be detected in their odors—they smell of smoke.

CHAPTER 1

Poltergeists Through the Ages

Over the centuries there have been many accounts of activities by poltergeists documented by witnesses and writers, but historians of the paranormal find most of them of dubious value. Since the study of the paranormal is a relatively new science, experts find many of these accounts unverified by independent sources. Moreover, many details have gone unrecorded: The dates, names of the people haunted by the poltergeists, many of the circumstances of the hauntings—all these facts and more were frequently omitted. Said Hereward Carrington, a British authority on the paranormal: "Many of them were so casually reported or inadequately observed that it is impossible to estimate their evidential value. A few of these were undoubtedly fraudulent, but many of them might well have been genuine—though the accounts failed to prove it!"[3]

Still, Carrington and other paranormal investigators have been able to dig far back into history to find dozens of bona fide cases of poltergeist hauntings. One of the first may have occurred in the year 355 A.D. in the German village of Bingen-am-Rhein. The case is regarded as significant because Jacob Grimm of the Brothers Grimm wrote about it in a book on German mythology. Wrote Grimm: "The unfriendly racketing and tormenting spirits who take possession of a house, are distinguished from the friendly and good-natured by their commonly form-ing a whole gang, who disturb the householder's rest with their riot and clatter, and throw stones from the roof at passers by."[4]

Blame the Poltergeist

Hundreds more cases would eventually surface, mostly in Europe, sparked largely by people's beliefs that good and righteous souls went to heaven and the souls of sinners went to hell, but some unfortunate souls were caught in between. These souls were left to wander the earth, caught in a netherworld between physical life and the paradise of heaven or the doom of hell. Wrote Catherine Crowe, a nineteenth-century author who first used the term *poltergeist* in describing these noisy spirits:

> There was . . . a midregion, peopled with in-numerable hosts of wandering and mourn-ful spirits, who, although undergoing no torments, are represented as incessantly bewailing their condition, pining for the life they once enjoyed in the body, longing after the things of the earth, and occupying themselves with the same pursuits and ob-jects as had formerly constituted their busi-ness or their pleasure.[5]

Therefore, if pictures fell off the walls or books flew off the shelves or stones fell from the sky—and there were no apparent and logical reasons for these strange and weird acts—people tended to blame a poltergeist. In her landmark book on the occult, *The Night Side of Nature*, Crowe wrote about a typical case: the 1654 haunting of the home of Gilbert Cambell of Glenluce, Scotland. The poltergeist damaged the Cambells' property, spoiled their food, and even tore their clothes as they wore them. In addition, the poltergeist spoke to the Cambells, although the spirit's words were evidently never recorded.

The Cambells endured the haunting for months. Finally, in October 1655 the frightened family turned to the Presbyterian Church for help. Ministers were dispatched to Glenluce, where they attempted to perform an exorcism, leading the entire population of the town in a day of prayer in an effort to cast out the haunting spirit. According to Crowe, this strategy produced mixed results: "Whether it was owing to this or not, there ensued an alleviation from that time to April; and from April to August they were entirely free, and hoped all was over, and they were dreadfully tormented through autumn, after which the disturbances ceased, and although the family lived in the house many years afterwards, nothing of the sort ever happened again."[6]

The Stone-Throwing Devil

The Cambell case proved that poltergeists could disappear as mysteriously as they appeared, giving the unfortunate human agents no warnings of their arrivals or departures. That was proved again a few years later in the town of New Castle in New Hampshire, where the farmhouse of George Walton was said to be haunted by a poltergeist. The Walton case is significant because it was among the first incidents involving poltergeist activity reported in America, and it was also one of the first incidents in which the evidence was thoroughly documented by a reputable witness.

During the summer of 1682, the Walton home was repeatedly pelted by stones, which evidently flew around inside the house as well as in an adjacent farm field. Also, several of the Walton family's possessions disappeared. The events at the Walton home were chronicled by a boarder, Richard Chamberlain, who happened to be the secretary to the New Hampshire provincial governor. Evidently, Chamberlain spent several sleepless nights with the Waltons, constantly awakened by the sound of stones pelting against the house, and was witness to many other strange occurrences as well. Chamberlain authored a pamphlet, which he titled *The Stone-Throwing Devil*, about his experiences with the Waltons, writing:

> On Tuesday Night (June 28) we were quiet; but not so on Wednesday, when the Stones were play'd about in the House. And on Thursday Morning I found some things that hung on Nails on the Wall in my Chamber, a Spherical Sun-Dial, etc., lying on the Ground, as knock'd down by some Brick or Stone in the ante-Chamber. But my Land-

Did You Know?
Sixty-four percent of poltergeist activity involves the movement of small objects, and 58 percent of poltergeist reports occur at night.

lord had the worst of that Day, tho' he kept the Field, being there invisibly hit above 40 times, as he affirm'd to me, and he receiv'd some hurtful Blows on the Back, and other Parts, which he much complained of . . . .

Besides this, Plants of Indian Corn were struck up by the Roots almost, just as if they had been cut with some edged Instrument, whereas they were seen to be eradicated, or rooted up with nothing but the very Stones. . . . And a sort of Noise, like that of Snorting and Whistling, was heard near the Men at Work in the Fields many times, many whereof I myself, going thither, and being there, was a Witness of; and parting thence I receiv'd a pretty hard Blow with a Stone on the Calf of my Leg.[7]

Did You Know?
Poltergeist activity is often at its strongest during new and full moons. Also, people should be wary of poltergeists in the days immediately preceding and following new and full moons.

Eventually, the poltergeist mysteriously disappeared, leaving the Walton family and their boarder to enjoy the peace and quiet of the New Hampshire autumn. According to Chamberlain, George Walton received the final blow from the poltergeist—he was struck in the head that September "with three pebble Stones as big as one's Fist; one of which broke his Head . . . the others gave him that Pain on the Back, of which he complained then, and afterward, to his Death."[8]

Flying Potatoes and Blaring Trumpets

The Waltons were menaced by flying stones, but a poltergeist could make anything fly: pots and pans, food, furniture, and whatever else in the house was not nailed down (and very likely, even if it had been nailed down, a poltergeist could rip the nails out and send that object flying as

OPPOSITE:
The belief that
righteous souls
go to heaven,
sinners go
to hell, and
some unfortu-
nate souls are
caught in be-
tween is illus-
trated by this
seventeenth-
century Italian
painting. Some
say that pol-
tergeists spring
from the neth-
erworld be-
tween heaven
and hell.

well). One had to be very careful in a house haunted by a poltergeist. Any object—an umbrella, a kitchen knife, even a chair—could be turned into a weapon.

A magician and actor named Walter Hubbell became frightfully aware of that fact when he dropped in on Daniel Teed and his family in Amherst, Nova Scotia. Living with the Teeds at the time was 18-year-old Esther Cox, whose sister Olive was married to Daniel.

On the night of September 10, 1878, Cox was visited by a poltergeist that swelled her body to twice its normal size and made her hair stand on end. The attacks continued for months. When a doctor was summoned, he was chased out of the house by a torrent of flying potatoes. A minister was chased away by the sounds of blaring trumpets. The Teed house was also plagued by loud booms, shaking furniture, and balls of fire that ignited on their own.

Hubbell heard about the case and thought he could cash in by putting Cox onstage. A modest shoemaker by trade, Daniel Teed favored the plan, believing Cox's share of the ticket sales could help the Teeds make ends meet, particularly since all this poltergeist activity had distracted Daniel from his customers. But when Hubbell presented Cox to an audience, the poltergeist refused to play any tricks, and Cox was booed off the stage. She returned to the Teed cottage, where the poltergeist's antics resumed.

Hubbell still believed he could find a way to make money from Cox's poltergeist and proposed to write a book about the case. He returned to the house, where he quickly found his life in danger. Hubbell explained:

> I had been seated about five minutes when,
> to my great amazement, my umbrella was
> thrown a distance of fifteen feet, passing
> over my head in its strange flight, and al-

most at the same instance a large carving knife came whizzing through the air, passing over Esther's head, who was just then coming out of the pantry with a large dish in both hands, and fell in front of her. . . .

I immediately left the room, taking my satchel with me to the parlor, where I sat down literally paralyzed with astonishment. I had only been seated a moment when my satchel was thrown across the room and, at the same instant, a large chair came rushing from the opposite side of the room, striking the one on which I was seated with such tremendous force that it was nearly knocked from under me.[9]

Hubbell went on to publish his book, while Daniel Teed finally had enough of Cox and her poltergeist. He kicked her out of the house. She found work at a nearby farm, but when the family's barn burned down, Cox was charged with arson. She served a month in jail, after which the visits of the poltergeist ceased and she was left alone for the rest of her life.

"Signs of Ill-Temper"

The case of Esther Cox set a standard for poltergeist visits that would be repeated over and over again: The human agent was often an adolescent girl or young woman. In the case of the Borley Rectory, the human agent, Marianne Foyster, was just 31 years old when she moved in to the old brick parsonage in Sudbury, England, with her husband, Lionel Foyster.

According to legend, the grounds of the rectory were the scene of an illicit love affair in the thirteenth

The White House Poltergeist

Many visitors, staff members, and residents of the White House in Washington, D.C., have claimed to have had encounters with the supernatural. Many have claimed to have seen the ghosts of President Abraham Lincoln as well as First Ladies Dolley Madison and Abigail Adams. Still others have encountered eerie noises and moving objects that sound more like the antics of a poltergeist. For example, President Benjamin Harrison assigned a guard to track down the intruder responsible for stomping loudly through the White House halls, keeping him up at night. The guard never found the culprit. When President Harry Truman lived in the White House, he was once awakened by a knocking on his bedroom door. When Truman opened the door, no one was there.

Gary Walters, a former White House chief usher, recalled:

> I was standing at the state floor of the White House adjacent to the staircase that comes up from the ground floor. The police officers and I felt a cool rush of air pass between us and then two doors that stand open closed by themselves. I have never seen these doors move before without somebody specifically closing them by hand. It was quite remarkable.
>
> We checked to see if there were some condition that may have caused the rush of air like other doors being opened or an air system starting and could find no evidence of any cause for the rush of air or the doors closing. This feeling of the passage of cold air has been related by other members of the staff through the years.

Quoted in The White House, "Ask the White House," October 31, 2003. http://georgewbush whitehouse.archives.gov.

century involving a monk and novice nun. When the affair was discovered, the monk was hanged and the nun bricked up inside a wall. In 1930 the Foysters moved in to the rectory with their two young children. They soon heard rapping noises and ringing bells while objects flew about the home. Marianne received the brunt of abuse from the poltergeist. She was slapped by invisible hands, thrown out of bed at night, and forced to dodge heavy objects seemingly aimed at her. One time she awoke to find herself being suffocated by her own mattress.

The case garnered the attention of Harry Price, England's most famous paranormal detective. Price hurried to the rectory, where he witnessed the abuse heaped on Marianne by the poltergeist. Price recalled:

> As Mrs. Foyster was walking along the passage outside the bathroom, she was struck by a terrific blow under the eye, resultant cut bleeding copiously. Though she was carrying a candle, she did not see what struck her. Her eye was black for some days. The next night, just as the Foysters had retired to rest, things started flying around the bedroom. A large cotton-reel that had stood on the mantelpiece was projected across the room; it struck the wall and fell on their bed. Then they felt something whiz by their heads and fall with a clatter to the floor. The rector lit a lamp and explored. The missile was a hammer-head.
>
> After some minor inconveniences—such as pins, with points upward, being found in the chairs the Foysters usually sat on—the "entities" began to show signs of ill-temper.

England's most famous paranormal detective, Harry Price, spent years investigating poltergeist activity at Borley Rectory (pictured). Among many bizarre events, Price wrote of objects being thrown at people or placed where they would trip over them.

> A favorite trick was to place things in passages and dark corners, where people would be likely to fall over them. . . . Mrs. Foyster tripped over a tin of bath salts that had been placed just inside the bathroom door. Then all went quiet for a few days—except, perhaps, for a little intermittent bell-ringing. [10]

Marianne moved out of Borley Rectory in 1933, leaving Lionel behind. She may have had enough of the poltergeist by then, but it is also likely that she had had enough of Lionel—who was 21 years her senior—because she moved in with a flower store owner. In any event, Lionel moved out of Borley Rectory in 1935, and four years later the haunted parsonage burned to the ground.

The Sad Case of Tina Resch

Among the saddest stories involving poltergeist activity and a young woman can be found in the case of Tina Resch, a teenage girl from Columbus, Ohio, who was believed to possess wide-ranging powers of psychokinesis. In fact, Resch's powers were so pronounced that she was able to levitate a telephone receiver as a news photographer snapped a picture. Meanwhile, the Resch house was subjected to various oddities—electric lights turned themselves on and off, the shower turned itself on and off, eggs flew out of the carton and smashed into the ceiling, pictures fell off walls, and knives jumped out of kitchen cabinets.

When William G. Roll, a University of West Georgia psychologist and paranormal investigator, looked into the Resch case, he suspected that a poltergeist may have been responsible for Resch's ability to levitate objects as well as the other strange occurrences. Roll described a typical meal in the Resch home:

> After Tina had come down for breakfast, [her mother] heard knocking from the front door. Before she could answer, she saw it was the candleholder on the wall in the hallway that was banging against the wall by itself. The six candles had already been broken or stored away, leaving the empty holder and the chain that held it in place. . . .
>
> Then a carton of apple juice on the counter by the sink sailed into the family room, smashing against the door to the garage. Juice spilled out everywhere. A picture in the hallway and a large picture over the couch in the living room swung back and forth on their nails. . . . Next the lamp on the

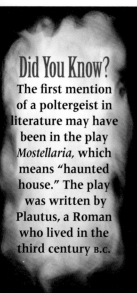

end table by the couch in the living room fell to the floor.[11]

The local press flocked to the home, providing Resch with a measure of celebrity. After the initial publicity over the Resch family poltergeist died down, Tina Resch faded into obscurity. Soon she entered into an unhappy marriage with a husband who abused her and stole her money. At first Resch and her young daughter, Amber, fled to a women's shelter, but then she moved in with another man, David Paul Herrin. In 1992 she contacted Roll and told him that the poltergeist had returned.

Before Roll had an opportunity to investigate, Resch found her name in the news again—but this time under much sadder circumstances: Amber, Resch's three-year-old daughter, had died from child abuse. Resch and her boyfriend, Herrin, were arrested and charged in her death, and both were sentenced to lengthy prison terms.

With Resch in prison, her poltergeist encounter has never undergone the scrutiny that Roll believes it merits. "I have been working on Tina's story for twenty years, and still I find much about her mysterious," says Roll. "But one thing is certain. For a time, Tina had the power to directly affect the physical world. I am convinced that this power is still to be found in the depths of her mind."[12]

Gilbert Cambell, George Walton, Esther Cox, Marianne Foyster, and Tina Resch all discovered just how malicious poltergeists could be—each emerged from their experiences battered and bruised. And although they all turned to members of the clergy or respected paranormal investigators to help rid them of their poltergeists, only the poltergeists themselves decided when it was time to leave and, perhaps, find other people to torment.

Did You Know?
Most poltergeist hauntings last between two weeks and a month. About a quarter of poltergeist hauntings persist for more than a year.

The Most Evil Spirits

There is usually nothing friendly about poltergeists. They can be mischievous, but they can also be malevolent. Poltergeists have terrified their victims. They have punched and pummeled people, tossed knives and heavy objects at them, set fire to their homes, and committed all manner of vicious acts.

People who have been roughed up by poltergeists have found it a very unpleasant experience. In 1612 a poltergeist paid a visit to the home of Francis Perrault, a Huguenot minister in the French town of Mascon. The poltergeist pelted Perrault and his family members with stones and was particularly vicious toward a young girl who worked in the house as a maid, pummeling her with invisible punches and repeatedly dowsing her with water even as she slept.

The so-called Devil of Mascon was also a chatty poltergeist. It is said that the spirit uttered the word *minister* over and over again, evidently to get Perrault's attention. In fact, Perrault carried on many conversations with the poltergeist, which told the clergyman about a murder that had occurred in the home when an angry wife pushed her husband down a flight of stairs. The poltergeist also seemed to know the darkest secrets of everyone who lived in the house or visited—it reminded Perrault that his father had been poisoned. On another occasion, the poltergeist made an appearance as Perrault entertained a friend. The poltergeist started speaking, which prompted the minister's guest to search about the kitchen for the source of the voice. When Perrault's guest thought he could detect the voice coming from a wine bottle, the poltergeist snapped, "I always heard you were stupid. Of course I'm not in the bottle!"[13]

As the case of the Devil of Mascon illustrates, the most evil poltergeists are often the chattiest poltergeists. Their threatening voices can often be heard as they heap abuse on their victims. Sometimes they do not speak but make other sounds—they may whistle, squeal like a pig, or croak like a frog. Their utterances are all intended to be pranks and frighten people.

Mary Ann Winkowski, a medium and paranormal investigator, says that she has occasionally sustained injuries when channeling evil poltergeists or otherwise making contact with the malevolent spirits. She adds that truly evil poltergeists are common, and people would do well to be wary of them, for they can be dangerous. She says:

> Dark entities, evil spirits, demons—whatever names they are given—have a lot of power. These are the forces that can move heavy pieces of furniture, tip over bookshelves, and kill or seriously injure pets or small animals. Some folks have told me about glimpsing shadowy black forms drifting through their homes. Others mention the unnerving appearance of blood-red eyes that seem to float in the darkness. Still other people have told me of spotted creatures with hooves, horns, or tails.[14]

Poltergeists are not believed capable of killing people on their own—although pets and other animals have

Did You Know?

Sixteen percent of poltergeist visits feature communication between the poltergeist and human agent; in 12 percent of the cases, doors and windows open and shut by themselves.

been slaughtered. And yet, the pranks played by poltergeists have often indirectly resulted in the deaths of their hapless victims.

The Bell Witch

One of the most well known cases of a poltergeist's pranks ending in tragedy occurred at the farm owned by John Bell of Robertson County, Tennessee. John and Lucy Bell were among the most prosperous families in the county—the parents of six children, they owned 1,000 acres (405ha), lived in a grand farmhouse, and kept slaves. There may also have been a dark side to the family—before buying the farm in Tennessee, John owned a plantation in North Carolina where he is reputed to have killed a man named John Black, possibly because Black had made romantic advances toward Lucy.

In 1818 the Bells started hearing strange scratching noises on the walls and doors. At first, they attributed the noises to rodents or tree limbs brushing against the house on windy days, but then the noises started sounding as though they were originating from *inside* the house. For several nights John and his sons conducted futile searches for the source of the eerie noises, traipsing up and down the hallways by candlelight. Each time, the Bells were forced to return to their beds, frustrated at their failure to find the source of the noises.

One night, just after returning to bed, the Bells' six-year-old son, Richard, was startled by the feeling that somebody was pulling his hair. "It felt like the top of my head had been taken off,"[15] he said later. The boy cried out in pain. The other family members rushed to his bedside; they tore the sheets and blankets from the mattress but found nothing.

Next to be attacked was Betsy Bell, aged 12. She felt

Did You Know?

Poltergeists are known to hurl objects through the house. Witnesses report, though, that the objects rarely travel in straight lines—most of them seem to curve, veer erratically, or float.

her hair pulled and cheeks slapped, sometimes so harshly that they would turn red and puffy. She often found herself poked, prodded, and punched. Meanwhile, other eerie occurrences were happening in the home—mysterious lights darted about the yard, bricks and scraps of wood seemed to fall from the sky. Soon stories spread throughout Robertson County about the strange events at the Bell house. Neighbors as well as strangers flocked to the farmhouse, anxious to catch a glimpse of what was now known as the "Bell Witch."

According to Richard Bell, many attempts were made to communicate with the Bell Witch, and some of them were actually successful. Richard recalled his parents and others carrying on conversations with the spirit, which replied to their questions in a whispered voice. During these conversations, the poltergeist identified itself as a number of people—a dead child, a dead Indian, a long-dead witch, and a newly dead neighbor named Kate Batts, who had been involved in a property-line dispute with John Bell. In fact, the poltergeist reserved its harshest and most punitive treatment for John, whom the whispering voice called "Old Jack."

The Death of Old Jack

At first John found a strange fungus growing on his tongue—at times, his tongue would become so swollen that he could neither eat nor speak. Next, he repeatedly felt as though he were being prodded by a pointed stick, often jamming into his cheeks. When a neighbor communicated with the spirit, asking why it was putting John through such painful turmoil, the poltergeist answered, "All you can know is that I will not leave until Old Jack Bell dies."[16]

The fungal affliction continued. So did the prods by the invisible sticks. John developed pains and twitches in

Did You Know?
Nuns who were visited by a poltergeist in 1598 reported that the spirit's method of torment was through tickling. Many of the nuns said they were tickled nearly to the point of death by the poltergeist.

his jaw and neck. By the summer of 1820, John's life had become intolerable—he was in constant pain, which had taken a toll on his health. No longer a robust and healthy farmer, John was frail and ailing.

On the morning of December 20, 1820, John's family could not wake him from his sleep. In a kitchen cupboard they discovered a near-empty bottle of poison; evidently, John had consumed the deadly potion and died. As family members gathered around John's bed, they heard the cackling voice of the poltergeist: "It's useless for you to try to revive Old Jack. I have got him this time; he will never get up from that bed again!"[17]

Although it would seem as though John's death should have satisfied the poltergeist, the Bell Witch is said to have returned to the farmhouse from time to time for another eight years—harassing members of the family, scratching on the walls, whispering threats, and occasionally playing pranks on the Bells. By 1828 only Lucy and two of her sons remained on the farm. She died that year. Her survivors divided up the land, tore down the farmhouse, and never heard from the Bell Witch again.

The Enfield Poltergeist

As the Bell Witch tormented John Bell and his family members, it constantly whispered its taunts and threats. Years later the so-called Enfield Poltergeist was just as chatty—and just as vicious in its attacks on Peggy Hodgson and her two daughters, Margaret and, especially, Janet. In 1977 the family chose to move in to a tidy home in Enfield, a suburb north of London.

The poltergeist activity started in the children's room when a chest of drawers started to slide across the floor under its own power. As the frightened children watched, the chest inched its way toward the door, evidently in

Did You Know?
An analysis of poltergeist visits concluded that most human agents suffer from either psychological or physical illnesses.

an attempt to block the entranceway into the room. Responding to the screams of her children, Peggy hurried to the room, managed to squeeze in through the narrowing doorway, and pushed the chest back across the room. As she released her grip, though, the chest started moving forward again. Peggy struggled against it, finding that the harder she pushed, the harder the chest pushed back. Finally giving in, Peggy released the chest, grabbed her children, and escaped through the doorway just seconds before the chest slammed against the door, closing off the exit.

The poltergeist soon returned to wreak havoc on the house. Along with the usual knocking sounds and flying books and other items, the poltergeist committed some major damage to the home by tearing a brick fireplace from the wall.

A brick fireplace, similar to the one pictured, was torn from the wall of a home in a London suburb in the 1970s. Paranormal investigators blamed the attack on a destructive poltergeist.

The Hodgsons were not the only ones to witness the poltergeist's activity. Over the next few months, they summoned friends, neighbors, and police officers to the home—more than 30 witnesses reported seeing paranormal activity in the residence. Peggy also summoned two noted London paranormal investigators, Maurice Grosse and Guy Lyon Playfair, to witness the eerie events. The two investigators spent many months in the home, and it was under their watch that the poltergeist's pranks turned decidedly evil.

Spinning Like a Top

Playfair and Grosse agreed to take turns staying up all night in the house to chronicle the poltergeist's activities. One night, on Grosse's watch, he heard screams coming from the children's room. He ran to the foot of the stairs, where he saw 12-year-old Janet being dragged through her bedroom door by an unseen force. Then she was hauled down the stairs, suffering painfully as her body was slammed to the floor at Grosse's feet. On a subsequent night, the poltergeist snatched Janet from her bed, then spun her wildly around as she hovered several feet in the air. Outside, a neighbor was stunned as she caught sight through the bedroom window of the young girl spinning like a top. "The lady saw me spinning around and banging against the window," Janet recalled years later. "I thought I might actually break the window and go through it. A lot of children fantasize about flying, but it wasn't like that. When you're levitated with force and you don't know where you're going to land it's frightening. I still don't know how it happened."[18]

When the spinning stopped, Janet fell back on her bed, but the poltergeist was not finished with her. Entering a trance, Janet started speaking in the poltergeist's

Andrew Jackson and the Bell Witch

Years before he ascended to the presidency, Andrew Jackson is believed to have encountered the Bell Witch while on a visit to the Bell farm. It is likely that John Bell was acquainted with the future president—he served under Jackson during the War of 1812. Moreover, during the years in which the poltergeist haunted the farm, Jackson practiced law in Nashville, about 35 miles (56km) from the Bell property.

According to witnesses, Jackson heard about the haunting and rode out to the Bell farm to investigate, accompanied by a medium who claimed he could channel the spirit. Jackson and the medium dined with the Bells, and soon the witch made its presence known. The poltergeist yanked on the medium's nose, dragging him across the room. Watching the commotion unfold in front of him, Jackson said: "By god, boys, I never saw so much fun in my life. This beats fighting the British."

Quoted in Michael Norman and Beth Scott, *Historic Haunted America*. New York: Tor, 1995, p. 469.

voice—it was a deep, gravely voice that identified itself as a man named Bill who had lived in the house some 50 years before. For the next several months, Janet often lapsed into Bill's voice, telling the horrified listeners of the events surrounding his death—he had died in the house, bleeding from the brain.

Janet and her family endured the visits of Bill the poltergeist for some two years. She was levitated often during that period and spoke again several times in Bill's voice. And then, quite mysteriously, Bill decided to leave the Hodgsons alone.

Although Janet and the other family members survived the encounter, they remain deeply disturbed by the haunting. "I felt used by a force nobody understands," says Janet. "I really don't like to think about it too much."[19]

Threatening Voice

For the Lutz family of Amityville, New York, the threatening voice of the poltergeist could be heard on the day they moved in to their new home in 1975. Just 13 months before the Lutzes acquired the home at 112 Ocean Avenue, it had been the scene of a horrific crime: 6 members of the DeFeo family had been brutally murdered by one of the DeFeo sons, Ronald. At his trial DeFeo pleaded not guilty by reason of insanity. He told jurors that he heard voices in the house that commanded him to kill his family. The jury did not believe his story, convicted him of 6 counts of murder, and sentenced him to life in prison.

The DeFeo family's survivors were anxious to be rid of the house. They found willing buyers in George and Kathy Lutz, who were able to obtain the property for several thousand dollars less than its value. Because of the house's gruesome history, the Lutzes asked a priest, Ralph Pecoraro, to bless the house. Pecoraro arrived to

Did You Know?

In most poltergeist visits it is not unusual for witnesses to relate vastly different stories about what they may have seen or heard.

find the Lutzes moving in. He made his way around the boxes and furniture, then began uttering a prayer while flicking drops of holy water onto the property. Suddenly, he heard a distinctive voice say, "Get out!"[20]

Pecoraro never mentioned hearing those chilling words to the Lutzes. Soon they would learn about the Amityville poltergeist on their own. Three days after moving in the Lutzes started hearing knocks on the doors and walls. Kathy felt the touch of an invisible hand. Odd odors of perfume and excrement emanated from the house. The Lutzes discovered cold spots in the house. They could hear doors slamming throughout the home. One morning George awoke to find the front door nearly ripped from its hinges. It appeared as though the door had been pried open from the *inside*—as though someone were trying to get out rather than break in. Recalled George:

> There were a number of times I would think a clock radio or something went off downstairs. I heard what I can only describe as a marching band tuning up, and at one time it had sounded like they had rolled up the carpet there were so many footsteps down there—there was so much noise. And you go running downstairs to see what it is or what caused this, and you get to the landing halfway down and there's nothing, and the dog would be asleep. At different times I can still remember looking at him and saying, "Some watchdog you're turning out to be."[21]

The events would soon grow eerier. Swarms of flies attacked the house. Kathy was levitated and spun around. She also suffered welts on her body. The Lutzes saw appearances by an apparition resembling a piglike creature with glowing red eyes. They also found cloven hoof prints in the dirt around the house.

For 28 days the family endured the taunts and pranks of the poltergeist. Finally, the Lutzes found themselves confronted by a pair of eyes hovering in their living room, staring at them. When Kathy hurled a chair at the eyes, they disappeared, but outside the Lutzes heard the sound of a squealing pig. The next day the Lutzes moved out—they fled to California, leaving behind their home, their clothes, and all their other possessions.

Was It a Hoax?

The Lutzes' story made international news. A best-selling book about their ordeal, *The Amityville Horror,* was published in 1977, followed by a hit movie in 1979 and a remake in 2005. Kathy Lutz died in 2004, and George Lutz died in 2006. Before their deaths the Lutzes were often forced to defend themselves against charges that the whole story was a hoax. Charges surfaced suggesting George Lutz cooked up the story with DeFeo's lawyer, William Weber—that Lutz hoped to sell the story, and Weber thought evidence of a poltergeist might help DeFeo win a new trial. The Lutzes steadfastly stood by their story, insisting that their home at 112 Ocean Avenue was haunted by a vindictive poltergeist—possibly the spirit of one of Ronald DeFeo's victims.

Before he died, George Lutz told an interviewer that a team of paranormal investigators explored the house in 1976 and concluded that the place harbored an angry poltergeist, and it was beyond their abilities to cleanse the home of the malevolent entity. Lutz said:

> What was there had never walked the face of
> the earth in human form, it was not going to

give up the house as such, and that it would have to be exorcised. As far as they were concerned, there was no more that they could do. . . .

So we left the house as it was, and I sold my business and we went on out to California and started over again. We left the house, all of our furniture and clothing and everything.[22]

Janet Hodgson and the young maid in the home of the Perrault family were fortunate—they survived the visits of the poltergeists, although not without bruises and, certainly, not without some very terrible memories. George and Kathy Lutz also survived their encounters with a poltergeist, escaping with their lives but sacrificing their savings and possessions. John Bell was forced to pay a much steeper price. For reasons known only to the poltergeist, the evil spirit that haunted the Bell home aimed to take John's life. The fact that the poltergeist ultimately succeeded serves as stark evidence that poltergeists can be noisy and mischievous but sometimes their intentions are truly evil.

Coroner's office staff remove one of six bodies found shot to death in a house in Amityville, New York, in 1974. Months later, the new residents reported frightening taunts and pranks that they attributed to poltergeists.

CHAPTER 3

Poltergeists in Person

Most people who claim to have seen poltergeists have not actually seen them. Instead, they have seen vases topple over and dishes hurtle through the air, or they have heard strange sounds. They may also have seen mysterious messages emerge on the walls, fires erupt spontaneously, or stones fall from the sky. From time to time, though, apparitions of poltergeists have been reported by witnesses.

At the former General Wayne Inn near Philadelphia, the proprietors and employees were aware for years that the place was haunted by a poltergeist. (Over the years, the restaurant was owned by several proprietors, but in 2006 it was purchased by a synagogue and converted into a Jewish community center.) During its history as a restaurant, many of the employees heard knocks on the walls and eerie voices and saw glasses and dinnerware vibrate. Employees of the inn learned to live with the paranormal events, believing them harmless. In a 1988 interview, the inn's former maître d' said, "Oh, you always heard banging on the walls, like creaking in the walls, lights flickering, the glasses shaking, wind—cold gusts of wind going past you real fast. It happened so often that we just . . . we eventually took it for granted. We just shrugged it off."[23]

However, the inn has something of a dark past. Dur-

The new owner of the General Wayne Inn describes his group's renovation plans. Employees of the former restaurant told of strange events occurring there, including eerie voices, creaking walls, flickering lights, vibrating glasses, and cold gusts of wind.

ing the American Revolution, a British regiment captured the inn and used it as a headquarters. One night soldiers of the Continental Army sneaked into the inn's basement, perhaps through a secret tunnel, where they surprised and killed a Hessian soldier—a German mercenary in the employ of the British—leaving his body hidden in the basement.

Eventually, the spirit of the Hessian made its physical presence known. One witness retrieving a box from the basement reported encountering a uniformed soldier in the basement. Later a restaurant hostess reported seeing the solider in the inn's dining room. The encounter lasted just a few seconds. "He had his hand on the railing and he sort of looked around and he looked startled, like he didn't know where he was," said the hostess in a 1988 interview. "And then as I was looking at him, he disappeared."[24]

As the case of the General Wayne Inn illustrates, poltergeists often take human form. But not always. Poltergeists aim to frighten, which means they can materialize in all manner of eerie images and shapes. They may appear as bursts of light or hazy phosphorescent clouds. And many times, what starts out seeming to be human soon morphs into apparitions that are truly monstrous.

Making Trouble

That is what eventually happened at the General Wayne Inn. At first, the occasional sighting of the uniformed Hessian soldier provided the inn with a quaint legend that was welcomed by the employees and proprietors—the poltergeist was good for business. Guests who dined in the restaurant were eager to hear eerie sounds or encounter other evidence of the poltergeist.

But poltergeists are known to be ornery spirits. They mean to make trouble and frighten people, and this particular poltergeist soon found a way to make mischief. Said the former maître d':

> We were closing the restaurant up for the night, and I was doing my usual walk through the kitchen to make sure everything was closed up and turned off. And as I was coming through one of the exit doors, I looked up and sitting on a chest of drawers that we have to keep the bread warm, I saw—just

for a split second—a head, just sitting there right on top of the [bread warmer]. And it was a very smoky color, as if it was a projection onto a screen or something. I only saw it for a second but I will never forget it.

It had a very painful expression . . . thin, slicked-back hair. His ears stuck out a bit. He had pencil thin eyebrows and a pencil thin mustache. And no neck or anything, just—just a head. That's all I saw. He was just sitting there, looking at me.[25]

Stunned, the maître d' hurried out of the room. He found a group of employees gathered around the bar and then blurted out, "I saw a head! I saw it!" Unable to compose himself, he was taken home by one of his coworkers. The ghostly image has remained imbedded in his mind for many years, giving him plenty of sleepless nights, which is, after all, the ultimate mission of a poltergeist. "I don't think it was a figment of my imagination," he insists. "I don't think it was a mirage. I saw something. I know I did."[26]

Did You Know?
Poltergeists may be drawn to a house because of a horrific crime committed there. They may be seeking justice, revenge, or some other way to find closure for what they consider unfinished business.

A Severed Arm

Centuries before the unfortunate maître d' of the General Wayne Inn encountered the severed head of the Hessian soldier's poltergeist, a visitor to the home of Scotsman Andrew MacKie found himself in similar circumstances. In this case, though, the witness did not catch sight of a severed head, but a severed arm that did not seem to be aware it was not attached to the rest of a body.

MacKie was a farmer in the town of Rerrick, Scotland. In 1691 MacKie found his home plagued by poltergeist activity in many of the usual ways. Stones were hurled at the house. Hot coals fell into the laundry, burning the family's clothes and igniting small fires. On one occasion, an iron bar used to lock the door sailed through the house as though it were a spear. A cooking pot flew across the kitchen. When MacKie retrieved it from the floor, it was yanked out of his hand by an unseen force.

The MacKie farm's poltergeist proved to be a particularly nasty spirit. MacKie and his visitors were occasionally whacked with wooden sticks and pelted with stones; his children were slapped in their sleep. Visitors had their feet yanked out from under them.

On the night of April 4, 1691, two ministers, Andrew Ewart and John Murdo, spent the night at the MacKie farmhouse with the intent of driving off the spirit with the power of prayer. Instead, Ewart was struck twice in the head by hurtling rocks, and Murdo was pummeled by unseen fists. Both ministers sustained injuries during their night in the MacKie farmhouse, and both left the next morning nursing their wounds. Their attempt at an exorcism had failed.

The apparition occurred when MacKie asked another minister, Alexander Telfair, to investigate the poltergeist's activities. While saying a prayer, the minister discovered an unusual sensation in his arm. "I felt something pressing up my arm," he wrote. "I, casting my eyes thither, perceived a little white hand and arm, from the elbow down, but immediately it vanished."[27]

A few weeks later, Telfair returned to the MacKie farm. Calling the MacKies and their friends into the barn, Telfair led them in prayer. Soon the assembled noticed a black cloud emanating from a corner of the barn. Within seconds the cloud expanded, surrounding everyone in the barn. Moreover, the black cloud seemed to kick up mud and hay, tossing dirt into their faces, while unseen hands gripped them by their waists. Telfair later wrote

Did You Know?

Some paranormal investigators do not believe that poltergeists are the spirits of dead people. Instead, they argue that poltergeists are eerie fields of energy that latch on to a person or house.

A British soldier (far left) watches as Hessian soldiers perform their duties during the American Revolution. Sightings of a uniformed Hessian soldier and other unexplainable events led General Wayne Inn employees to conclude that the restaurant was haunted by a poltergeist.

that some people felt the cold hands of the poltergeist on their hips for several days following the prayer meeting in the barn. "It was affrighting to them all," wrote Telfair, "that some said, for five days thereafter they thought they felt these grips: after an hour or two of the night was thus past, there was no more trouble."[28]

The Return of Susannah and Oliver

Andrew MacKie and his family never discovered whose severed hand may have touched the arm of their minister. As with most poltergeists, the Rerrick spirit left as mysteriously as it had arrived. Other poltergeists that have made physical appearances have provided clues to their identities. In many cases their faces are as familiar as the faces found in nearby paintings and photographs.

In 1857 Susannah Plowden, a young woman from Cockeysville, Maryland, committed suicide after her family banished her new husband from the household. Despondent over her family's refusal to accept her husband, Plowden hanged herself in the hayloft in the barn on the family's plantation. The only image of Plowden to survive was an oil painting rendered of her shortly before her death, depicting a young and beautiful red-headed woman dressed in a white dress and blue sash.

The Plowden house was located on a slave-owning plantation. Following the Civil War the house fell into disrepair. Over the next several decades, many of the Plowden descendants drifted away, and the dark story of the death of Susannah Plowden escaped from local history.

A century after Plowden's death, the house was purchased by the Simonson family, who loved old homes and intended to restore the house to its pre–Civil War grandeur. The Simonsons invested a great deal of money and energy into the old home, and they soon found themselves the proprietors of a stately property reminiscent of the era of the Old South.

Unfortunately, the Simonsons also soon found themselves enduring poltergeist activity. Plowden's former room was continually cold and drafty—the Simonsons retained an engineer, who was unable to find the source of the draft. The family's cats were curious animals that seemed constantly underfoot, but the cats stopped in their tracks at the threshold of Plowden's room, refusing to enter.

Elsewhere in the house, kitchen cabinets fell off the walls. Photographs and paintings dropped from their hooks. One painting, a portrait of a young woman hung in Plowden's room, constantly flew off the wall. Finally, the Simonsons attached the portrait to the wall with bolts. When they were out of the room, they heard a loud crash. Running into the room, the couple found that despite the bolts, the picture had been ripped from the wall and cast on the floor.

Finally, the poltergeist emerged in physical form—two houseguests who spent separate nights in Plowden's room reported seeing the apparition of a young woman wearing a white gown and blue sash—the image a close match to a portrait of Susannah Plowden owned by an ancestor.

Determined to get to the bottom of the mystery, the Simonsons retained a medium, who organized a séance. As the medium drifted into a trance, she started uttering the name "Oliver" over and over again. That was all the Simonsons had to hear, for soon after they had moved in to the home, they discovered an old diary in the attic. It did not take much reading to learn that the diary had belonged to Plowden—in its pages, the sad and tragic girl described her marriage, her family's hostility to her new husband, and her plans to take her own life. They also knew from reading the diary that

Did You Know?

William G. Roll, the psychologist and paranormal investigator, found that in more than 100 poltergeist cases he had studied, 27 included apparitions.

Oliver was the name of Plowden's banished husband.

One more eerie incident stands out in the case of the Simonson house. After moving into their new home, the Simonsons took photographs of all the rooms. In one of the pictures, a faint image of a man is clearly visible. The Simonsons were never able to determine the identity of the face in the photograph. Was it Oliver searching for his beloved Susannah? That question remains unanswered.

The Poltergeist of President Garfield

Sometimes it does not take much detective work to learn the identity of a poltergeist, because the apparition is that of a well-known person. In Hiram, Ohio, the spirit of former president James A. Garfield is said to still occupy his former home. Garfield's apparition has appeared from time to time, usually preceded by an abundant amount of poltergeist activity.

Since Garfield's death, the house has had several owners. Over the years, many strange events have occurred there: electric lights that turned on and off by themselves, including lamps that were not plugged into electrical outlets, and faucets that gushed water even when the taps were off. On one summer day, one of the hottest on record, the owners came home to discover the house as cold as a freezer. Moreover, candles seemed to jump out of candleholders on their own, then explode. Doors would often swing open and closed by themselves.

In 1961 the home was purchased by a schoolteacher, Bruno Mallone, and his wife, Dorothy. One morning Bruno retrieved the morning newspaper, then sat down to solve the crossword puzzle over breakfast. When Bruno opened the paper, he discovered that somebody had already solved the puzzle. When the Mallones investigated, they discovered the handwriting in the puzzle

A Furry Poltergeist

One of the more famous poltergeist cases on record occurred in 1931 when James T. Irving, a farmer on the Isle of Man off the coast of Great Britain, claimed to have been visited by a poltergeist that took the form of a mongoose. The furry little poltergeist, which Irving named Gef, talked to the farmer but also, in fits of anger, pelted the farmer and his family with stones, hurled objects around the kitchen, and seemed to be most active in the presence of the farmer's teenage daughter, Voirrey.

Hungarian paranormal investigator Nandor Fodor heard about the case and hurried to the island to see for himself. Fodor stayed in the Irving home for several days, combed the property, and traipsed across the island, but he never encountered Gef. Still, he left the island convinced that there was substance to Irving's story and later wrote about the case in a book on the paranormal. "That the 'something' which is called Gef exists and talks, I hold proved," he declared, "but as to what it is, opinions may differ. Once we step into the marvelous, reason and logic give us no bearings."

Quoted in Cliff Willett, "Investigating Gef: Pt 3," Gef: The Eighth Wonder of the World. http://dalbyspook.110mb.com.

appeared similar to the handwriting of President Garfield. Moreover, the Mallones often smelled cigar smoke in the home. Bruno did not smoke cigars, but the couple was aware that Garfield had enjoyed cigars.

Actually, it should not come as much of a surprise that Garfield may have returned to his old home in spirit form. As a young man Garfield was very interested in the supernatural. He had lost his father as a young child, and as an adult made many attempts to communicate with him through mediums. Some of those séances were held at his home in Hiram. Also, Garfield had a premonition about his own death—years later, he died from an assassin's bullet, murdered by a disgruntled office seeker.

Convinced that the house was haunted by the spirit of the nation's twentieth president, the Mallones made an attempt to gather evidence. They often ran a tape recorder in an effort to capture the president's words. One time their tape machine picked up the words of a man speaking a language they did not recognize. (What made the incident particularly eerie is that the Mallones did not hear the speaker with their own ears—only the machine picked up the words.) When Bruno took the tape to the foreign language department of a nearby college, he was told the voice was speaking Greek. From their research, they knew that President Garfield was conversant in Greek. On another occasion, the Mallones retained a medium. Channeling the former president, the medium—who was right-handed—used her left hand to write out the words, "I am James Garfield. . . . I am unhappy because so-called friends had me murdered."[29] Garfield, the Mallones learned, was left-handed.

President Garfield's poltergeist finally made an appearance. Before dawn one morning Dorothy was awakened by the movement of a tall man in the bedroom. Thinking it was Bruno, she asked him if he planned to go back to bed. Then she realized Bruno had already left for school that morning. As for the poltergeist of President Garfield, it vanished an instant later.

Looking Like Real People

Sometimes poltergeists can look uncannily like ordinary people. Medium Mary Ann Winkowski claims to be able to see spirits that are invisible to others, and on occasion she has seen poltergeists at work.

On one occasion Winkowski stopped at a diner with her husband, Ted. While waiting to be served, Winkowski caught sight of a spirit engaging in some typical poltergeist mischief: He was turning the coffeemaker on and off, frustrating and angering the waitresses. "He was a huge guy, maybe in his forties, wearing the white T-shirt and work pants that you might see on a line cook or counter help," she said. "His arms were covered with tattoos, and he had a crew cut and a mean glint in his eye."[30]

Later, as one of the waitresses emerged from the kitchen carrying the Winkowskis' dinner, Mary Ann saw the poltergeist following close behind. Said the medium, "I watched as he tipped the back end of her tray up until our dishes and dinner crashed to the floor."[31]

As the experiences of Andrew MacKie, the Simonsons, the Mallones, and the employees and guests of the General Wayne Inn would appear to indicate, poltergeists are more than just entities that can make books fly off shelves, dishes fall from cabinets, and eggs break on the floor. Poltergeists can also manifest themselves in some truly frightening apparitions, forcing the unfortunate people who see them to remember those unforgettable images for many years.

Hunting Poltergeists

For Marc and Marianne Fallon, life started getting strange soon after they moved in to their new home in South Shields, a coastal town in northeast England. One night, during the summer of 2006, as Marc and Marianne prepared for bed, their young son Robert's toy dog suddenly flew across the room, just missing Marianne's head. Other toys became airborne as well. The frightened couple tried to hide under their blanket, but unseen hands tugged at the fabric—Marc and Marianne had to struggle against the mysterious force trying to pull the blanket off the bed.

Seconds later, the tugging stopped—but then Marc cried out in pain. His back seemed to be on fire. As he took off his shirt, his horrified wife saw claw marks on his back—it appeared he had been attacked by a vicious beast. "Marianne," he cried, "my body feels like it's burning. What's happening to me?"[32] And then, as mysteriously as the claw marks surfaced, they went away.

For months the Fallons endured similar strange events in their home. Toys came alive again, acting like missiles as they flew across the room. The toilets often flushed themselves—after the bowls filled with blood. Threatening text messages appeared by themselves on the couple's mobile phones. "I was too scared to sleep and too frightened to stay awake," said Marianne. "I felt we

Did You Know?

Some poltergeists have been cast out by religious prayers spoken by members of the clergy. In most cases the poltergeists seem to leave on their own.

just couldn't escape from it. No matter what we did, we couldn't get away."[33]

Was the Fallons' home haunted by a poltergeist? With nowhere else to turn, the Fallons hired two paranormal investigators, Mike Hallowell and Darren Ritson, to get to the bottom of the mystery.

Throughout the home Hallowell and Ritson set up video cameras, motion detectors, sound sensors, and other detection devices. Incredibly, within days of initiating the investigation, Hallowell and Ritson recorded an apparition on a video camera. "The entity walked slowly from the bathroom, across the landing in the bedroom," said Hallowell. "As it passed the door to Robert's room, it paused and stared icily at me. Its face, devoid of all features such as eyes, nose or mouth, was cold and menacing. It felt like it was burrowing into my soul."[34]

As the work of Hallowell and Ritson appeared to show, some very sophisticated electronic eavesdropping equipment, including cameras and audio recording devices, can help detect poltergeist activity. Hallowell and Ritson are not the only ones who seem to have an ability to root out poltergeists.

Did You Know?

A study of poltergeists by British paranormal investigator Guy William Lambert found that in half of the 54 cases he reviewed, the hauntings occurred in houses located within 3 miles (4.8km) of rivers or oceans. Further, he found that in most cases the poltergeists made their appearances during rainy, foggy, or snowy conditions.

Electronic Equipment

There are dedicated amateurs around the globe who chase down sightings of ghosts and poltergeists. In many cities paranormal enthusiasts have formed clubs and make the news from time to time when they turn up evidence of paranormal activity. A few ghost hunters have gone on to author books about their discoveries and develop national reputations.

Actually recording an apparition on camera, which Hallowell and Ritson say they were able to do, is rare. In most cases paranormal investigators look for other

Two ghost hunters try to detect and record signs of ghostly activity in an Iowa opera house, using various devices, including a video camera. Cameras and electromagnetic field detectors are commonly used ghost-hunting tools.

evidence they say will prove the existence of poltergeists.

At Bucksville House, a bed-and-breakfast in Kintnersville, Pennsylvania, owners Joe and Barbara Szollosi have endured the pranks of a poltergeist since they bought the inn in 1983. In this case the Bucksville House poltergeist has been more of a nuisance than a terror. The spirit likes to hide tools and other household implements as well as the guests' possessions—hiding a guest's shoe is a favorite prank. "We had a guest who came back to her room and said, 'My shoe was on my pillow. Did anybody put my shoe on my pillow?'" recalled Barbara Szollosi. "The next day, she came downstairs and as she was leaving, she told us her shoe is missing."[35] Elsewhere in the inn doors occasionally slam shut by themselves, and the checkers on a checkerboard are often found out of position, even though no one has touched the board. In one of the bedrooms, the fire in the fireplace is known to start on its own, without being ignited.

Reports of paranormal activity at the inn raised the interest of the Philadelphia Ghost Hunters Alliance, whose members showed up one evening armed with cameras and other recording devices. Many of the devices employed by the group are available in electronics stores. For example, some members of the group used electromagnetic field detectors to test the electrical and magnetic fields that many believe accompany poltergeist activity. The detectors cost between about $20 and $200 and are used mostly by utility workers to test cables and transformers found at electrical power plants. (Cables and transformers that leak electromagnetic power are believed to cause cancer, so utility companies test them constantly to ensure they are properly insulated.) "Electromagnetism is one of the things we try to test [for] when we go on an inspection," said Lew Gerew of the Philadelphia group. "Some people believe spirits are electromagnetic in origin."[36]

Digital recorders as well as tape recorders are handy, of course, to capture raps and other sounds made by poltergeists. Night-vision goggles can be useful as well. They enable people to see in low-light conditions—the type of atmosphere many poltergeists prefer. Thermometers are used to take the temperature of the house. Since cold spots are often found in houses where there is poltergeist activity, thermometers have detected wide varieties of temperatures throughout the homes under inspection. Gerew said his group has found room-by-room temperature dips of as much as 60°F (16°C). "[Poltergeists] draw energy from heat in the room," he said. "That would create a cold spot in the room."[37]

Cameras are frequently employed in poltergeist searches. Paranormal detectives use digital cameras as well as film cameras, often using infrared film. Infrared film records images that emit infrared radiation, which emanates from heat-producing objects. In other words, if a poltergeist draws heat from the room, infrared film may be able to capture an image of that ball of energy.

On the other hand, digital cameras have the advantage of enabling the photographer to see the image instantly after taking the picture. Therefore, if the photographer is

Did You Know?
The accumulation of water is a common sign of a poltergeist. Often water will drip from unusual places and form puddles. Typically, the reaction of the homeowner will be to call a plumber, but when the plumber investigates, he or she never finds a leaky pipe.

lucky enough to snap a picture capturing an apparition or energy field, the other equipment can be immediately employed to capture the sounds, temperature and electromagnetic energy of the poltergeist.

Catching Orbs

About a half dozen members of the Philadelphia Ghost Hunters Alliance took part in the investigation at the Bucksville House. Their hunt started on the first floor, which includes the inn's parlor and kitchen. The paranormal detectives spent several minutes taking temperature readings and digital photographs, concluding that no evidence of poltergeist activity could be found in those rooms. The team then decided to move on to the second floor, where most of the inn's guest rooms are located.

Soon the search started turning up evidence of paranormal activity. In one of the second-floor guest rooms, a digital camera recorded images of "orbs," which experts believe are tiny balls of energy that indicate the presence of a paranormal entity. The image displayed in

A soldier demonstrates the use of night-vision goggles. While soldiers use the goggles to search for enemy aircraft, ghost hunters use them to spot poltergeists in low-light conditions.

the camera showed a hazy ball of light. Other members of the alliance fired the shutters on their digital cameras as well, and soon most of the cameras caught images of orbs—many of the objects appeared to be baseballs streaking across the room. Meanwhile, temperature readings were taken in the guest room; the alliance members found the temperature to be 10°F (12°C) cooler than in the other rooms of the house.

During the hunt another club member took a seat in an antique rocker. Suddenly, she announced that her hands felt cold. Instantly, the alliance members fired off digital photographs. As they examined the images, none of the alliance members were surprised to discover that they had photographed an orb hovering over their friend's hands.

Later, in a report Gerew filed on the alliance's investigation of the Bucksville House, he said: "It was almost sitting directly on top of her hands. Almost all of the investigators present that night were in the room to see this first hand. Truly amazing. . . . Based on the photographic experiment alone, it is my belief that there is at least one spirit that inhabits the Bucksville Inn."[38]

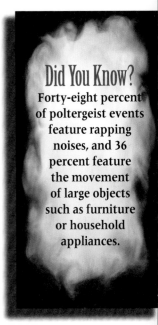

Did You Know?
Forty-eight percent of poltergeist events feature rapping noises, and 36 percent feature the movement of large objects such as furniture or household appliances.

Send for the Exorcist

The members of the Philadelphia Ghost Hunters Alliance produced results on their equipment, but in many instances even the best equipment has failed to record poltergeist activity. In the Enfield case a reporter and photographer from a newspaper were summoned. During their visit, toys started flying through the air, and one even struck the photographer in the head. The photographer took many photographs of the weird occurrences, but when the film was developed, the photos showed no poltergeist activity.

Evidently, poltergeists can control cameras and other recording equipment when they want to. Therefore, it may become necessary to find a medium who can make contact with the poltergeist, usually through a séance. At the Bucksville House, a medium conducted a séance, concluding that the poltergeist in residence was the spirit of a girl named Sarah who lived in the house 200 years ago.

The Bucksville House poltergeist was not a malevolent spirit, so there was no need to drive it away. As has been shown, though, poltergeists can often be noisy, ornery, and dangerous, and it may be necessary to retain the services of an exorcist. Dating back to at least biblical times, exorcism is used to drive off evil. An exorcism is typically performed to drive off a demon, which is an agent of the devil that may have possessed a human soul. Exorcists have also been called in to cast out other entities, including malevolent poltergeists, that haunt individuals or their homes. An exorcist can be a member of the clergy or somebody else familiar with the incantations and rituals required to drive off an unwanted spirit. If a Catholic priest is called in, he will utter a prayer that was first written in 1641. The prayer is intended to cast a demon from the soul of a person, but the prayer has been used to expel poltergeists. Otherwise, many mediums feel they are qualified to conduct an exorcism. They usually repeat incantations they have drawn from a number of sources, such as folklore or the writings of mystics and psychics.

In Easington, England, Sabrina Fallon—no relation to Marc and Marianne Fallon—hired a local medium, Suzanne Hadwin, to exorcise a poltergeist after Fallon and her two children had endured months of paranormal activity. Soon after moving into their home in 2007, the Fallons were constantly terrorized by banging noises, slamming doors, and bedclothes floating about the house on their own. "I called the police one night suspecting that it may be thieves but they couldn't find anything

and suggested it might be ghosts," said Fallon. "It was then that I called Suzanne for help."[39]

Hadwin channeled the ghost, learning that the home had been the scene of a grisly murder some 50 years before. She also learned that the poltergeist, which was named Peter, had the most evil of intentions. The spirit hoped to possess the soul of Fallon's 16-month-old daughter, Amy, so that it could relive its life.

To drive off the poltergeist, Hadwin laid down a circle of salt around the house. Salt has long been regarded as a symbol of purity and has been used for centuries to protect homes against witches, ghosts, poltergeists, and other evil entities. She also used prayer and religious symbols. "I got rid of the poltergeist by laying salt circles in the house as areas of protection for the family," said Hadwin. "I then used the power of prayer, sprinkled holy water and called in some angels to take the spirit to the place he needed to be taken."[40]

Home Remedies

Medium Mary Ann Winkowski counsels victims of poltergeist activity that there may be a few techniques and home remedies they can try on their own to rid their homes of unwanted paranormal visitors. Winkowski also advocates surrounding the house with salt. She finds sea salt to be more effective than table salt for cleansing a property of poltergeist activity. Also, she finds the seeds from a fruit known as a quince—which is similar to an apple or a pear—are effective. Human agents who are terrorized by poltergeists find that if they carry quince seeds in their pockets, the poltergeists often stay away.

Many herbs and wildflowers are also effective in driving off poltergeists. Winkowski recommends lighting a bundle of the herb sweetgrass, then blowing it out so

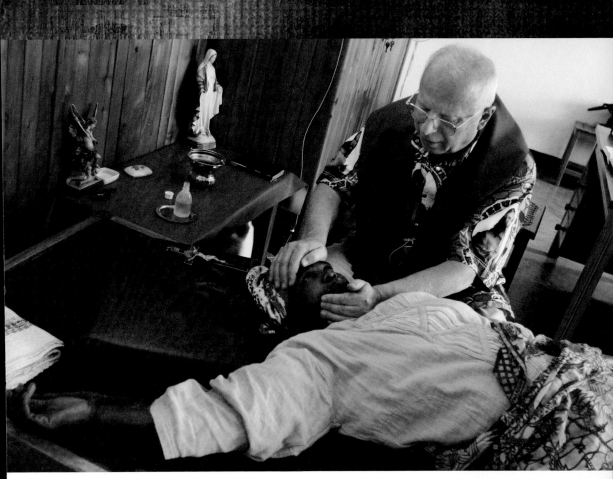

A woman who believes she is possessed undergoes an exorcism in the Democratic Republic of the Congo. The ceremony, intended to cast out spirits, is performed by a Catholic priest.

the plants continue to smolder. (She warns people to be careful as they light the sweetgrass to prevent fires from starting.) The smoking plants are taken from room to room, where they can leave their odor behind. She calls this "smudging" the house. "Start in the attic, if you can, and end in your basement," says Winkowski. "If you have an attached garage, don't forget to smudge there. Be sure to smudge behind doors, in corners, in closets, and in cabinets. If the smudge stick goes out—and it will if there's a lot of negative energy in the house—relight it and continue smudging from the spot where it first went out."[41] The human agent should also be sure to come into contact with the sweetgrass smoke.

Smudging a house offers a temporary solution—it may only keep the poltergeist away for a few days. Therefore, it may be necessary to repeat the smudging. Other herbs and plants are also helpful. For example, Winkowski has found that a garland of marigolds strung across a doorway may help keep a poltergeist out of the house. Geraniums dried and placed in the corners of basements may be an effective home remedy. Smearing oil from the myrrh tree in rooms where poltergeist activity has been strongest may help cast out the spirit. The herb rosemary can be sprinkled around the perimeter of the home—some people find it is more effective than salt. Some people find that carrying a violet with them provides protection from poltergeists. Winkowski says:

> I will admit right now that I don't know exactly why certain things work to diminish the energy of earthbound spirits. For instance, I cannot tell you exactly why the quince seeds my family sends me from their small village in Italy prevents ghosts from entering buildings. But I can tell you from my experience that they absolutely do work. Because they work for me, I have faith in their power and so I use them.[42]

The work by groups such as the Philadelphia Ghost Hunters Alliance shows that some paranormal investigators take a scientific approach to investigating poltergeist activity—they show up armed with cameras, audio recorders, thermometers, and other high-tech equipment. Others take a more homespun approach—Suzanne

Poltergeists That Will Not Leave

When it comes to getting rid of poltergeists, noted English ghost hunter Harry Price did not put much faith in exorcisms. "Parenthetically, I will say a few words about exorcisms. They are very seldom effective, or, if so, only temporarily. They seem to annoy the entities," said Price. "I have cited many cases where priests, Anglican and Roman Catholic, have exorcized—or attempted to exorcize—the disturbing 'spirits.' Practically all were failures."

Price recalled the case of Ada M. Sharpe of the town of Tackley, England. After enduring poltergeist activity from 1905 to 1908, the woman turned to the Anglican Church for an exorcism. L. de Clare performed the ritual. "The atmosphere of the house immediately changed, and all was quiet—until the following January," Price wrote. "Then, Miss Sharpe 'heard a dog walking round her bed.' Later, she could not close her bedroom door because something on the other side was pushing against it. Then she found a 'form' huddled up in bed." According to Price, Miss Sharpe asked another priest to perform an exorcism, and this time it worked.

Harry Price, *The End of the Borley Rectory.* Warwickshire, England: Read Books, 2006, p. 53.

Hadwin relies on her powers as a medium as well as some old-world and religious remedies, including the use of salt and holy water, to identify and drive off the evil spirits. Most people haunted by poltergeists would probably agree that any method employed to get to the truth about poltergeists is worth trying.

CHAPTER 5

Some Simple and Some Not So Simple Explanations

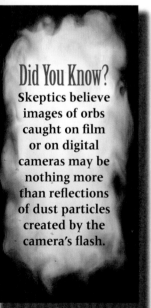

In October 1998, 50 residents of the town of Delain, France, gathered to set up the auditorium of the village church for an orchestral concert. As they worked inside, strange events started unfolding before their eyes. Suddenly, candlesticks flew through the air. Vases and statues crashed to the floor. "Believe me, I'm not someone who's really interested in the supernatural," said the mayor of Delain, Thierry Marceaux, "but when you see it in front of you . . ."[43] Terrified, the townspeople of Delain summoned a Catholic archbishop, who was asked to exorcise the church of its poltergeist.

The archbishop, Max de Wasseige, arrived a few days later and conducted a prayer service, which seemed to work. Actually, the archbishop could have stayed home. The police had also been looking into the case of the Delain poltergeist and concluded that the culprit was not a spirit from beyond, but Mayor Marceaux.

Evidently, the mayor was just having some fun with his constituents. Working alongside the other villagers in the church the night of the poltergeist's visit, the mayor waited until everyone turned their backs, then tossed the candlesticks across the room. Later he lurked in the shadows, knocking over the vases and statues. Finally, Marceaux appeared with the others and feigned surprise at the poltergeist's antics. Police elected not to charge the

mayor and instead let him go after he promised to seek psychiatric counseling.

Most skeptics of the paranormal insist that there are plenty of logical explanations for the activities of poltergeists. Some of those explanations include the perpetration of hoaxes. Other explanations may involve misunderstandings of normal and very explainable events by people who seem more ready to accept supernatural causes than more rational explanations—such as the weather, or leaky pipes, or mice living in the walls. But some experts say there may be more complicated reasons, some involving a breach of the laws of physics they cannot fully explain. Indeed, the phenomena that result in poltergeist-like activities may bridge the gap between the natural and supernatural. Says paranormal investigator William G. Roll: "Physics is considered the bedrock on which other sciences rest and to which they can ultimately be reduced. This bedrock is not as solid as it once seemed."[44]

Society of Skeptics

The citizens of Delain thought they saw statues falling and candlesticks soaring across their church hall and automatically accepted the notion of a poltergeist without seeing the need to investigate further. Others who witness what at first blush seems unexplainable are a bit more willing to be skeptical and search for explanations before summoning mediums and exorcists.

In Italy a homeowner placed a carved crystal panda on the top of a wardrobe in his apartment. The next morning, the owner noticed that the panda seemed to have moved a few inches. How was that possible? The owner moved the panda back to its original place, but the next morning he again found the panda seemed to have taken a few tiny steps on its own. He even drew a circle around the panda's base, then checked a third morning and found that the crystal figurine had moved beyond the circle.

The owner suspected that something in his apartment was causing vibrations, and therefore the movement of the panda, but after carefully examining his TV and stereo equipment, he concluded that nothing could be jostling the panda out of position. And then one day he saw the panda move on its own.

Resolving to get to the bottom of the mystery, the panda's owner rigged his apartment with sound sensors. In 2005, Italian paranormal investigator Massimo Polidoro reported the true cause for the "poltergeist" activity:

> These sensors respond to an interruption of a magnetic field, such as those produced by household appliances. He suspected, in fact, that the movement was caused by an appliance in one of the neighboring apartments. He was right: the cause of the "poltergeist" was finally found to be the new super-silent washing machine in the apartment upstairs![45]

Did You Know?

A study by Wright State University in Dayton, Ohio, found that houses where paranormal activity is alleged to have occurred take as much as 50 percent longer to sell than other houses. Moreover, their sale prices are 2.4 percent lower than similar homes on the market.

It May Be Just a Feeling

People who believe in poltergeists and other eerie beings may simply be reacting to the tension they feel in the room, according to a 2003 study by the University of Hertfordshire in Great Britain. Researchers for the university took a group of study participants to Hampton Court Palace in England and the South Bridge Vaults in Scotland—two allegedly haunted places. Some of the participants knew about the haunted histories of the two locations, but some did not. In both places many of the participants claimed to hear footsteps, feel cold spots, or sense the presence of supernatural beings in the rooms with them—regardless of whether they knew the places were supposedly haunted.

The researchers theorized that the gloom and tension that hung over Hampton Court Palace and the South Bridge Vaults were primarily responsible for producing the reactions among the study participants. "Hauntings exist, in the sense that places exist where people reliably have unusual experiences," said Richard Wiseman, a psychology professor who helped lead the study. "The existence of ghosts is a way of explaining these experiences."

Quoted in Arran Frood, "Ghosts 'All in the Mind,'" BBC News, May 21, 2003. http://news.bbc.co.uk.

Polidoro is among the ranks of paranormal specialists who investigate claims of poltergeists and other eerie activities with an eye toward disproving them. He is a regular contributor to the magazine the *Skeptical Inquirer*, which is published by the Amherst, New York–based Committee for Skeptical Inquiry (CSI). Founded in 1976, the group was originally known as the Committee for the Scientific Investigation of Claims of the Paranormal. Among its founders were some of the most distinguished scientists of the era, including astronomer Carl Sagan, paleontologist Steven Jay Gould, and biologist Richard Dawkins. "We were interested in criticizing the distortions in the media of alleged phenomena, from the psychics and UFOlogists to astrologers and faith healers," says Paul Kurtz, a former philosophy professor at the University of Buffalo and chair of the group. "These posed, in our view, a threat to the integrity of science, for they fudged the differences between genuine science and pseudoscience."[46]

A Teenager's Prank

Over the years, CSI has helped shed light on many alleged paranormal incidents, including supposed visits by poltergeists. In 2005, Polidoro recalled one case in which mysterious fires were igniting in a home. The family could not find the source of the blazes and, rather quickly, suspected the cause may have resided outside the laws of nature. Polidoro was called in to investigate, and his suspicions were soon drawn to a young daughter in the house. "It turned out that her mother had announced that a little sister was on the way, and the girl was not at all happy about it," said Polidoro. "Somehow, she had found a lighter around the house and used it to set fire to the curtains, clothes, and blankets—to the horror of the parents. The

Did You Know?

Although digital images as well as prints made from negatives are easy to fake, photography experts find that it is extremely difficult to alter images caught on negatives. Therefore, orbs, apparitions, auras, and other eerie images captured on film are often regarded as real.

An astrologist works with a star chart. Members of the Committee for Skeptical Inquiry expose astrologers, psychics, UFOlogists, faith healers, and others who they believe blur the difference between genuine science and pseudoscience.

whole family finally decided to consult a psychologist and was able to overcome its problems."[47]

Another case that CSI followed closely unfolded in 1997 in Emeryville, Ontario, Canada. For months Debbie and Dwayne Tamai had been menaced by a mysterious and harassing voice on their telephone. The voice, which called itself Sommy, did much more than just make threatening calls. Somehow Sommy was able to cut in on the Tamais' conversations when they were speaking with other people. He had access to the Tamais' voice mail number, even changing the personal identification code without their knowledge. He was also able to change the ring tones on their home phones.

The Tamais tried all manner of solutions to keep Sommy off their phones. They summoned technicians from the phone company, who rewired the house several times. Thinking that Sommy had planted eavesdropping equipment in the house while it was under construction, the Tamais had several of their walls ripped open but found no hidden devices. When producers from the NBC News program *Dateline* learned of the incidents, they dispatched a team of electronic security experts to sweep the Tamai house. But the *Dateline* team also found nothing. After the electronic sweep, Sommy called Debbie Tamai and laughed. "He told me I can get the best people in the world to come in my home and they won't find anything," she said. "I'm waiting for the one person to come and tell me, 'I've found something.'"[48]

Reporters started wondering whether Sommy may be a poltergeist, but CSI was skeptical. "Unfortunately, *Dateline* failed to enlist the real ghostbusters," declared CSI research fellow Joe Nickell. "Some of us at the headquarters [of CSI], and no doubt elsewhere, formed a hypothesis as soon as we saw the program. We realized that many of the phenomena described, such as the eavesdropping, could have been accomplished more easily by someone in the house."[49]

Nickell also suspected that the harassing phone calls had something of an adolescent flair to them—and so did the local police. After interviewing the Tamais' 15-year-old son, Billy, several times, the police finally concluded that the boy had been making the harassing phone calls to his parents the whole time. The fact that Billy Tamai was something of an electronics whiz, enabling him to avoid detection by the telephone company technicians and security experts who were called in, may have helped enhance the belief that the calls were the work of a poltergeist, but in the end it was simply a teenager's prank.

Faking Photographs

Cameras have been capturing paranormal images since the earliest days of photography in the mid-nineteenth century. Melvyn Willin, a professor of criminology at Cambridge University in Great Britain, has sifted through hundreds of photos of ghosts and poltergeists and has concluded that most of them were faked. At the time they were taken, though, many people believed what they saw. Willin suggests that people at this time were more willing to accept the images in the photos because they were more apt to believe in the paranormal.

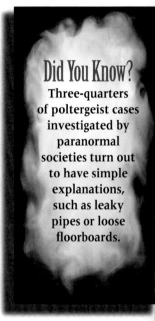

Did You Know?
Three-quarters of poltergeist cases investigated by paranormal societies turn out to have simple explanations, such as leaky pipes or loose floorboards.

Meanwhile, the craft of photography—which was still in its infancy—was not understood by most people, who were not aware that photographers could perform many manipulations of their images in their darkrooms. "Many of the photographs from this era are now known to have been faked, but were so sincerely believed to have been genuine at the time that they are of interest to us," says Willin. "It was an age when belief in the afterlife was almost universal, and an unexpected windfall from the new invention of photography was that it seemed to prove this."[50]

Today images of orbs and other paranormal activities captured by digital cameras are constantly met with skepticism by critics who point out that anyone with a computer and photo retouching software can alter a digital photograph, placing an orb, apparition, or hazy aura in a picture with just a few simple keystrokes. "Unfortunately, there are some unscrupulous individuals who perpetrate these allegations by creating 'doctored' and fake photos and present them as real," says paranormal investigator Janice Oberding. "Since skeptics are capable of producing fake orb photos that are almost identical to a genuine orb photo, it has been suggested that all orb photography be dismissed as everything but ghosts."[51]

Explainable Events

While it can be easy enough for a prankster to alter a few digital photographs to perpetrate a hoax, not all fake poltergeist visits are created through subterfuge. Some alleged poltergeist activity is due simply to the desirability of witnesses to accept supernatural explanations for otherwise explainable events. For example, it may not be out of the question for a poltergeist to slam a door shut, but it is more likely that the wind blowing through an open window is the real culprit. And while a pool of water forming on the floor is often regarded as evidence of poltergeist infestation, the residents of the haunted house would probably do well to call a plumber before seeking the services of an exorcist.

Poltergeists are often blamed for hurling darts of lightning. Many witnesses describe balls of fire that have streaked across rooms or outdoor locations, such as farm fields. For nearly 150 years, residents of Warren County, Iowa, have been convinced their community is haunted by a poltergeist who tosses lightning bolts at farmers and others at the most unpredictable times. One farmer, Orval Benning, said he saw streaks of lightning as he walked home from a late-night card game. "That light was no more than twenty-five feet in front of me," he said. "There was no moon and there was no one in the field with a lantern. "[52] Another farmer, Roy Whitehead, even reported

Did You Know?

In a study by paranormal investigator William G. Roll, 92 of 116 poltergeist cases involved a single human agent in which Roll suggested the probable cause of the activity was recurrent spontaneous psychokinesis. In 56 of the 92 cases, the human agents were girls or young women.

A ghost hunter sets up a night vision video camera in an effort to document paranormal activity along a section of reportedly haunted railroad track in Ohio. Skeptics dismiss most photos and film of ghostly activity, arguing that they are easy to fake.

that the lightning bolts made sounds, describing what he heard as "the cry of a lost earthbound soul."[53]

Scientists suggest that so-called ball lightning is a bizarre but explainable phenomenon. Over the years there have been some 10,000 reported sightings of ball lightning, which forms due to a buildup of electricity in the air, usually ahead of a thunderstorm. When the electrical energy comes into contact with the moisture in the air, it manifests itself as a glowing orb. The Royal Society, which is Great Britain's national academy of science, conducted a study of ball lightning, reporting the story of one witness who described the formation of an orb of energy the size of a basketball outside a house. Seconds after forming, the huge orb shot into the home through a screen door—a circumstance that one might mistake for the prank of a poltergeist. In another case chronicled by the Royal Society, a Russian man reported that a ball of lightning bounced off his head before disappearing— again, an account that could certainly be confused for the antics of a poltergeist. In fact, scientists have created ball lightning in the laboratory.

Emotional Tension

Still, not all poltergeist activities are so easily explained. No matter how hard the wind may have blown through an open window, it probably did not blow hard enough to move the chest of drawers in the Enfield case. And no amount of wind was likely strong enough to hurl potatoes at the unfortunate doctor who came to the assistance of Esther Cox. Some paranormal investigators have looked into these incidents and others and have concluded that they are not due to visitations by poltergeists, but by the phenomenon known as recurrent spontaneous psychokinesis, or RSPK.

Paranormal investigators say RSPK is sparked by the welling up of emotional tension often found in girls and young women, who, not coincidentally, make up a majority of the human agents in poltergeist cases. It is also true that others have found themselves the targets of poltergeist activity. Experts believe anyone is capable of summoning the powers of RSPK if they are in the proper emotional state. In simple terms the human agents at the center of poltergeist cases are often going through crises in their lives. They may have had emotional breakups with their boyfriends or have suffered the losses of loved ones through death. The emotional tension that surfaces during an RSPK episode manifests itself by emitting energy that causes objects to fly across rooms, matches to ignite by themselves, pictures to fall off walls, and other events to occur that are otherwise blamed on poltergeists. Says paranormal investigator William G. Roll, who originally developed the theory of RSPK: "If an emotionally charged object has been freed of gravity and inertia, the object may levitate. The role of the RSPK agent would be twofold, to cause a brief cancellation of the gravity and inertia of the object . . . and to direct energy to the object

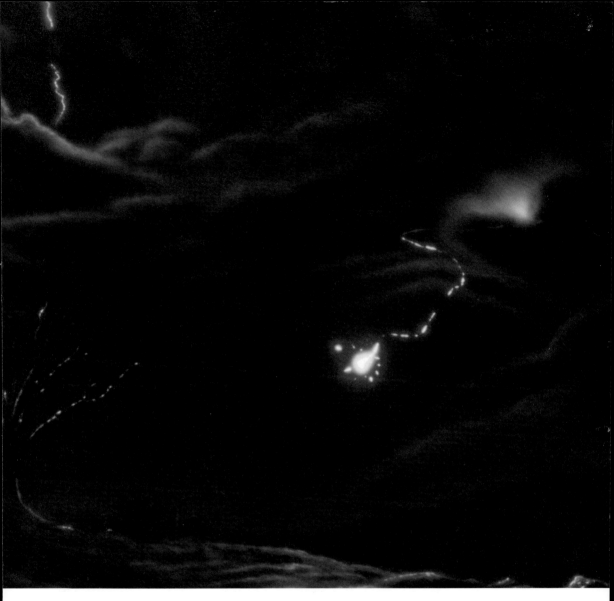

Ball lightning, depicted in this illustration, is thought by some to be a sign of poltergeist activity. Scientists say it is actually a buildup of electricity that often develops just before a thunderstorm.

for it to move."[54] Under this theory there is no ghost in the room—the poltergeist's mischief was caused not by the soul of a long-dead prankster but by the heartache of a teenage girl who has just broken up with her boyfriend.

RSPK energy may have been behind a 1961 case in

which the poltergeist activity plagued Edith Berger, a young woman from Long Island, New York, whose fiancé had recently died. Within minutes of learning of her fiancé's death, Berger felt herself violently pummeled by the spirit of her late boyfriend. One time the poltergeist grabbed her hair, giving it a painful yank. Berger's mother was also physically abused by the boyfriend's poltergeist. The Bergers endured these events for four months, then contacted a medium who attempted to cast out the spirit through an exorcism. The effort failed; soon after the medium concluded her work, the violent attacks on Berger and her mother resumed. Moreover, apparitions of the dead fiancé also began to appear to Berger.

Finally, the family called in paranormal investigator Hans Holzer, who counseled Berger to get over her emotional attachment to her dead boyfriend. "I . . . explained to her that she had to sacrifice—rid herself of her own desire to have this man around, unconscious though it may be—and in closing this door on this chapter of her life, make it impossible for the earthbound one to take control of her psychic energies."[55] Once Berger was able to rid her heart of the love she felt for her dead fiancé, the RSPK episodes ceased.

Real and Verifiable

Are poltergeists real? Certainly, there are pages and pages of documented evidence of poltergeist activity. The records show that many competent individuals have been witness to eerie events they cannot otherwise explain. And despite the charges of skeptics who claim they are nothing more than hoaxes, there are still plenty of photographs, video recordings, audio recordings, temperature readings, and other scientifically gathered evidence that stand up to close scrutiny, suggesting

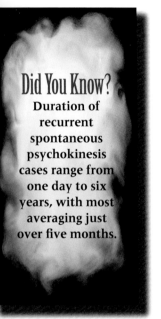

Did You Know?
Duration of recurrent spontaneous psychokinesis cases range from one day to six years, with most averaging just over five months.

poltergeist activity is real and verifiable.

The first reports of poltergeists surfaced nearly 2,000 years ago. Since then a lot of skeptics have provided ample evidence to prove that poltergeists are merely the products of overimaginative minds. But the skeptics have yet to convince everyone that poltergeists are myths—particularly those unfortunate people who have been pelted by stones, seen fireballs shoot across their living rooms, heard eerie voices, or been grasped by the cold and invisible hands of the poltergeist.

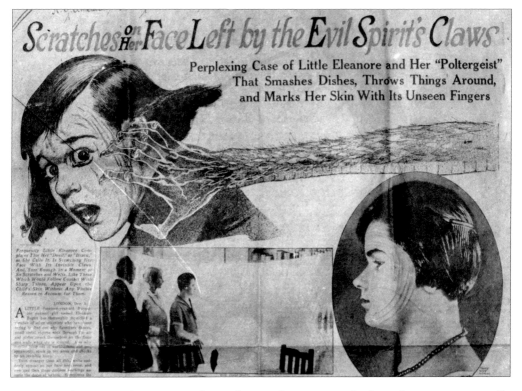

Many poltergeist hauntings have been documented though not necessarily proven. A 1926 New York newspaper features the bizarre story of a poltergeist that smashed dishes, threw things, and scratched the skin of a girl known as "Little Eleanore."

Source Notes

Introduction: What Is a Poltergeist?

1. Brian Righi, *Ghosts, Apparitions and Poltergeists*. Woodbury, MN: Llewellyn, 2008, p. 121.
2. Quoted in Tracey Lawson, "Sicilian Fires Recall Nanny 'Witch' Ordeal," *Scotsman*, February 12, 2004. http://news.scotsman.com.

Chapter 1: Poltergeists Through the Ages

3. Hereward Carrington, *Haunted People: The Story of the Poltergeist Down the Centuries*. New York: Dutton, 1951, p. 17.
4. Jacob Grimm, *Teutonic Mythology, Vol. 2* London: George Bell & Sons, 1883, p. 514.
5. Catherine Crowe, *The Night Side of Nature; or, Ghosts and Ghost Seers*. New York: Dutton, 1904, pp. 1–2.
6. Crowe, *The Night Side of Nature*, p. 431.
7. Quoted in George Lincoln Burr, *Narratives of the Witchcraft Cases, 1648–1706*. New York: Charles Scribner's Sons, 1914, pp. 71–72.
8. Quoted in Burr, *Narratives of the Witchcraft Cases, 1648–1706*, p. 76.
9. Walter Hubbell, *The Great Amherst Mystery: A True Narrative of the Supernatural*. New York: Brentano's, 1916, pp. 100–101.
10. Harry Price, *The End of Borley Rectory*. Warwickshire, England: Read, 2006, pp. 49–50.

11. William G. Roll and Valerie Storey, *Unleashed: Of Poltergeists and Murder: The Curious Story of Tina Resch*. New York: Pocket Books, 2004, pp. 11–12.
12. William G. Roll, "Tina Resch: Unleashed," *Fortean Times*, December 2004. www.forteantimes.com.

Chapter 2: The Most Evil Spirits

13. Quoted in P.G. Maxwell-Stuart, *Ghosts: A History of Phantoms, Ghouls, and Other Spirits of the Dead*. Gloucestershire, England: Tempus, 2006, p. 108.
14. Mary Ann Winkowski, *When Ghosts Speak: Understanding the World of Earthbound Spirits*. New York: Grand Central, 2007, p. 175.
15. Quoted in Michael Norman and Beth Scott, *Historic Haunted America*. New York: Tor, 1995, p. 461.
16. Quoted in Brent Monahan, *An American Haunting: The Bell Witch*. New York: St. Martin's, 1997, p. 79.
17. Quoted in Norman and Scott, *Historic Haunted America*, p. 471.
18. Quoted in Danny Penman, "A Suburban Poltergeist," *Daily Mail*, (London), March 5, 2007, p. 34.
19. Quoted in Penman, "A Suburban Poltergeist," p. 34.
20. Quoted in ABC News, "Amityville Horror: Horror or Hoax?" October 31, 2003. http://abcnews.go.com.
21. Quoted in Jeff Belanger, "George Lutz's Amityville Horror," Ghostvillage, April 12, 2005. www.ghostvillage.com.
22. Quoted in Staci Layne Wilson, "Exclusive Interview with George

Lutz and Dan Farrands—Part Two," Horror.com, April 9, 2005. www.horror.com.

Chapter 3: Poltergeists in Person

23. Quoted in Michaeleen C. Maher, "Quantitative Investigation of the General Wayne Inn," *Journal of Parapsychology*, December 2000, p. 370.

24. Quoted in Maher, "Quantitative Investigation of the General Wayne Inn," p. 369.

25. Quoted in Maher, "Quantitative Investigation of the General Wayne Inn," p. 371.

26. Quoted in Maher, "Quantitative Investigation of the General Wayne Inn," p. 371.

27. Quoted in Maxwell-Stuart, *Ghosts,* p. 156.

28. Alexander Telfair, "A True Relation of an Apparition, Expressions and Actings, of a Spirit Which Infested the House of Andrew MacKie," National Center for Supercomputing Applications, University of Illinois at Urbana-Champaign, December 2, 1695. http://norma.ncsa.uiuc.edu.

29. Quoted in Norman and Scott, *Haunted America,* p. 280.

30. Winkowski, *When Ghosts Speak,* p. 206.

31. Winkowski, *When Ghosts Speak,* p. 207.

Chapter 4: Hunting Poltergeists

32. Quoted in Danny Penman, "Objects Flying Through the Air, Mysterious Claw Marks on a Man's Skin, and Vicious Death Threats . . . Left by a Ghost," *Daily Mail,* (London), May 22, 2008, p. 32.

33. Quoted in Penman, "Objects Flying Through the Air, Mysterious Claw Marks on a Man's Skin, and Vicious Death Threats . . . Left by a Ghost," p. 32.

34. Quoted in Penman, "Objects Flying Through the Air, Mysterious Claw Marks on a Man's Skin, and Vicious Death Threats . . . Left by a Ghost," p. 32.

35. Quoted in Hal Marcovitz, "Could They Be Ghosts? Bucksville House Has a Face in a Fireplace, Photos with Strange Glows, a Mischievous Shoe Thief and a Man in a Black Hat," *Allentown* (PA) *Morning Call,* October 31, 1997, p. B-1.

36. Quoted in Hal Marcovitz, "A Scientific Method Used to Find Ghosts," *Allentown* (PA) *Morning Call,* February 8, 1999, p. B-1.

37. Quoted in Marcovitz, "A Scientific Method Used to Find Ghosts," p. B-1.

38. Lewis Gerew, "Bucksville House B&B," Philadelphia Ghost Hunters Alliance, February 16, 1999. www.phillyghost.com.

39. Quoted in Paul Sims, "Send for the Exorcist!" *Daily Mail,* (London), February 12, 2008, p. 19.

40. Quoted in Sims, "Send for the Exorcist!" p. 19.

41. Winkowski, *When Ghosts Speak,* p. 218.

42. Winkowski, *When Ghosts Speak,* p. 211.

Chapter 5: Some Simple and Some Not So Simple Explanations

43. Quoted in *Deseret News,* "Freaky Happenings Prompt Villagers to Call

for Exorcist," October 22, 1998. http://archive.deseretnews.com.

44. William G. Roll, "Poltergeists, Electromagnetism and Consciousness," *Scientific Exploration,* 2003, p. 80.

45. Massimo Polidoro, "Beware of Poltergeists," *Skeptical Inquirer,* September/October 2006, p. 22.

46. Paul Kurtz, "New Directions for Skeptical Inquiry," *Skeptical Inquirer,* January/February 2007, p. 7.

47. Polidoro, "Beware of Poltergeists," p. 22.

48. Quoted in David Crary, Associated Press, "High-Tech Harassment Stalker Menaces Family," *Bergen County* (NJ) *Record,* August 15, 1997, p. A-23.

49. Joe Nickell, "The Electronic Poltergeist," *Skeptical Inquirer,* September/October 1997, p. 12.

50. Melvyn Willin, *Caught on Film: Photographs of the Paranormal.* Cincinnati: David & Charles, 2007, p. 10.

51. Janice Oberding, *Haunted Nevada.* Boca Raton, FL: Universal, 2001, p. 106.

52. Quoted in Norman and Scott, *Historic Haunted America,* p. 161.

53. Quoted in Norman and Scott, *Historic Haunted America,* p. 162.

54. Roll, "Poltergeists, Electromagnetism and Consciousness," p. 83.

55. Hans Holzer, *Ghosts: True Encounters with the World Beyond.* New York: Black Dog & Leventhal, 1997, p. 625.

For Further Research

Books

Gary Leon Hill, *People Who Don't Know They're Dead*. Boston: Weiser, 2005.

John Kachuba, *Ghosthunters: On the Trail of Mediums, Dowsers, Spirit Seekers, and Other Investigators of America's Paranormal World*. Franklin Lakes, NJ: New Page, 2007.

P.G. Maxwell-Stuart, *Ghosts: A History of Phantoms, Ghouls, and Other Spirits of the Dead*. Gloucestershire, England: Tempus, 2006.

Michael Norman. *Haunted Homeland*. New York: Forge, 2006.

Harry Price, *The End of Borley Rectory*. Warwickshire, England: Read, 2006.

Brian Righi, *Ghosts, Apparitions and Poltergeists*. Woodbury, MN: Llewellyn, 2008.

William G. Roll and Valerie Storey, *Unleashed: Of Poltergeists and Murder: The Curious Story of Tina Resch*. New York: Pocket, 2004.

James Van Praagh. *Ghosts Among Us: Uncovering the Truth About the Other Side*. New York: HarperOne, 2008.

Melvyn Willin, *Caught on Film: Photographs of the Paranormal*. Cincinnati: David & Charles, 2007.

Mary Ann Winkowski, *When Ghosts Speak: Understanding the World of Earthbound Spirits*. New York: Grand Central, 2007.

Internet Sources

BadGhosts, "Marianne Foyster—the Dark Lady of Borley Rectory." http://badpsychics.co.uk/badghosts/modules/news/article.php?storyid=77.

Richard Chamberlain, *Lithobolia, or The Stone Throwing Devil*, Emerson Baker, History Department, Salem State College, http://w3.salemstate.edu/~ebaker/chadweb/lithoweb.htm.

Web Sites

The Amityville Horror (www.amityvillehorror.com). The Web site chronicles the case of George and Kathy Lutz, whose home in Amityville, New York, was terrorized by a poltergeist. The site includes several interviews with the late George Lutz, who spent years defending his story against critics who charged that he had perpetrated a hoax. The site also includes the stories of other witnesses and investigators who support Lutz's contention that the poltergeist was real.

Committee for Skeptical Inquiry (www.csicop.org).
Web site of the Amherst, New York–based group founded by scientists to

debunk accounts of poltergeists, ghosts, unidentified flying objects, and other examples of the paranormal. Visitors to the Web site can read past articles from the committee's magazine, the *Skeptical Inquirer,* and visit the Skeptiseum, an online museum of phony evidence offered by witnesses as proof of the paranormal.

Ghost Hunters
(www.scifi.com/ghosthunters).
Companion Web site to the Sci-Fi Channel's weekly series *Ghost Hunters.* The series follows the activities of the Rhode Island–based Atlantic Paranormal Society. Visitors to the Web site can see videos in which team members provide explanations of their techniques for investigating paranormal activity and display the equipment they use. Deleted scenes from episodes can also be viewed.

Harry Price: Ghost-Hunter, Psychical Researcher & Author
(www.harryprice.co.uk).
The life and work of British paranormal investigator Harry Price is chronicled on this Web site, which includes excerpts from several of Price's books. Visitors to the site can find summaries of Price's cases, including his long and thorough investigation of the Borley Rectory poltergeist.

Philadelphia Ghost Hunters Alliance
(www.phillyghost.com).
Visitors to the Web site can read the alliance's reports on its visit to Bucksville House as well as other historic places in Pennsylvania said to be haunted, including the Betsy Ross House, Fort Mifflin, and the General Wayne Inn. Students can also read about orbs, how photos can be faked, and find out the dates of the alliance's next investigations.

Univ-Con (www.univcon.org/index.php).
Web site for Univ-Con, the annual conference of paranormal enthusiasts. Each September, more than 500 enthusiasts attend the conference at State College, Pennsylvania, where they can hear lectures by experts, tour nearby haunted places, and attend workshops on how to conduct paranormal investigations. Visitors to the Web site can read highlights of past conventions, find a directory of American paranormal groups, and read essays by conference participants on issues related to paranormal study.

Index